D1522276

THE
HERO
PONY

Also by David Mamet
Published by Grove Weidenfeld

THE HERO PONY

Poems
by

David Mamet

GROVE WEIDENFELD
New York

Published by Grove Weidenfeld
A division of Grove Press, Inc.
841 Broadway
New York, NY 10003-4793

Published in Canada by General Publishing Company, Ltd.

Library of Congress Cataloging-in-Publication Data

Mamet, David.
    The hero pony : poems / by David Mamet. — 1st ed.
        p.   cm.
    ISBN 0-8021-1221-8 (alk. paper)
    I. Title,
 PS3563.A4345H47   1990
 811'.54—dc20   90-48467
                                                    CIP

Manufactured in the United States of America

Printed on acid-free paper

Designed by Irving Perkins Associates

First Edition 1990

10 9 8 7 6 5 4 3 2 1

to R.

Contents

THE
HERO
PONY

Tippu
Tib

Tippu Tib was a slaver chief
Who wrought out his unhuman brief
Down Madagascar way.

O'er luckless souls with dusky skins
He laid his plans and set his gins
Back in the Slavery days—

That sultry hell where he was host
To the hapless niggers of the Barbary Coast

Where pirates pledged their misery
In a deep huzzah in a minor key
That stole through the thickened haze.

So then thank God for your tidy home,
And your safe remove from the briny foam
That ran to Tippu's judgment seat;
Where the pirates laughed at the hammer beat—
When the smith forged shackles on your feet;
And, torn from the eyes of your family,
You were transported across the sea
To dwell in perpetual slavery.

Then go to sleep and sleep the night
And God protect you till the light,
In your quiet home in a quiet land
Surrounded by those who, doubtless, can
Protect you from Tippu Tib.

Jews. March 1989

Who else, in that case, could it have been?
No one. Indeed, it was not.
Those faces, cigarettes,
The publication of a novel.
Hot tea, steaming beyond hot,
And wretched-tasting.
How one loved it. Forty-
Year old memories.
Gratefully lost.

We thank you. In our shame.
The ghastly
Pendulum swing of our race
Who would not trade it if we could—
Knowing that we cannot.

Nothing but Good

Don't go up.
Those things
That
Or which
You should
One said
"Nothing but good."

But kept on
The once and
Strength avails
A contravention of
That ambiguity
The like
Those ills

The remedy
Is not in conquest
But alone
In the
Rebirth.
Rather proclaim it
Fear to the converse
Nothing but good.

A Poem on Easter Sunday

10,000 couples in the park.
No irony lessens the ill
That hard eyes utter.
"We are together now,"
And we are blessed.
Our love is butter
And the world is bread.
Then how could we distill
The wish from out the vow?
And we will know no rest
Until we walk that walk
And have done what we said.

Poem

Wet Janus
Back and forth.
That's the womb of the sea.
And that
Is our most placid car.

A man stood on the steamer and he said
Be safe.
You rode it. Never came to grief.
You never can.

Years later, live in the Z.I.
He saw he was that man.

What in the
Horror of war,
Stain of an unspent life?
One moment. Warmed by Irony. Perceived
A ferry boat.

The Office

In the office of the creator
Walked by the marble stair
I stood before
The mailchute in awe
That men who had gone before me
Had had the love and thought
To harness gravity,
To have prepared a perfect and
An ordered society.
If only he would come
Out from behind his desk
And take me home.

Janus

Cursed to accept in the day
As in himself, complete decay;
In a dead afternoon
That sheared off half the face of Janus.
With a retrograde glance, then,
You could proclaim
But you could not exult in proclaiming
That you endorse in the very naming
Those things which your little victories of perception
Cause to be.
This life, then, no mistaken tragedy,
And yours no choice to graciously submit:
You are not martyred by the thing you see,
You were conceived to hasten it.

June

June and its influence
Are coming in;
And the dull sense
Of ending.
Resolve to begin
What has begun
Will not suffice.
Not "a will bending,
A task to be done."
Just a stunned notice.

The Young Heroes

They have fulfilled their task.
Now we can find
Their picture on the wall.
That they have been
Abstracted from the dross
Is all we ask.
So one can stand for all.
And self-revulsion
Held time-out-of-mind
For one instant abates.
Our fealty demonstrates
We go to any length
To show that, although crucified
We, through our dying strength
Have raised the cross.

The Joke Code

You can take any of it
And take it at any point
And out of it
Extrapolate the whole—
From the half-fossil
To the newspaper advert
Lining a hatbox.

Work of twenty years
Not worth
One woman who
Could not stop shaking,
Gripped by pleasure
And it would not wane

Except that I am writing.

An odd dream
In a killing room.
God's ambiguity,
One final application
In this otherwise shithole
Of a chuckling shambles.

In a Dressing Room

Once a four-minute pause graced,
Or if it did not grace
Th'report, held true,
flattered our vanity.

And, elsewhere, weakness, too,
like those good niggers—
Basest secrets
everyone knew.
But we had toiled so
to claim the privilege.

Oh, to grow old in it
drunken and vomiting,
wrench the cloak,
draw up, and stride
in that elitist dawn.

Cafe

Sick fags
Poor benighted fags
Oh, fags
Oh, denizens of
Brightest day
No half-tones
No upon the
Staten Island
Ferry nights
Left with the
Company of Women
Talked of work
Left with the night
Chose immaterial
Not even fabric but
Food. Poor considerations

People:
What is gesture
And what if you
Would ask for
Someone must if
Not he said
You then I what

Is obeisance and to
What?
Who's conquered
habitude
Not I not you
And not I and not you.

Ode

But I do it all
But I would like
To do none of it.
Nor the disease
Ravaged and fearing
Left
With the excision only.
Or a fevered
You could not say kiss
It was a kiss
You sought
And no compliance.
That love gift
A thickened ode to death.

Two Men

A red hand on the horse's flanks
One hundred-and-some years ago
In these same precincts
In a yellow shirt
Dog warriors bet on
The absence of a Gatling Gun.
Some called on God and some
On Colt's Repeating Pistol
Patented Eighteen Seventy Three.
We know who killed him and why.
But a spy said to me
"You would have made
A good Marine."
While we sat in my kitchen drinking.
And he told me
Who killed Kennedy.

Winter

Fatigued by the tea
A cold sweat
Tired my body.

The grey
Will not dissipate at dusk.

It has arisen.

However we pray
It will not rise again.

One sick Jew
In a cold room
In the last days of the Jews.

The New House

Clean sheets in a warm room.
Patches where you tore your clothes.
Tools wear—we become fond of them.

Wood furniture or floors where we have nicked it
Makes the truest history.

The New House becomes The Old House.
The children move away
And decades later there is a knock at the door.

You say,
"I wonder if I might come in. I used to live here."

Lights move up the ceiling—headlights of the cars.
The color of the walls is changed.
The way my father held me that night
When I was so sick . . .

But I remember
The mark in the closet floor
And nights I heard my lovely house.
So quiet.
A voice, then another voice
In the next room.

And all that long time that there was the smell of paint.
  Then it was gone.

An old man at the door says,
"Do you think I could come in?
I used to live here."

One April 1988

What was it?
Something became lodged in the machine.
That was it.
Which inflection would not cure.
A tenuous hold much worse
Than no hold at all.
Who braved that consignment
And who braved that fall
Learned in the solitude
Of a white sickroom—
What choice had they
But not to resist?
You love that texture of a sheet
And you will pay for it.
So sweet, so sweet, he said,
Then, don't stop.
No stop for it.
Why.
A carnival.

The Fish

The fish, the fish,
You understand,
That came out of the sea
Came out on the land
And said "Grant me my wish."
You said that you were to be
The recipient—how odd—
And not the grantor. How could he not see
The formula had been inverted
"But, no," he said,
"Heaven-sent I am.
Then bend the knee
To one who, though dim is your understanding
You may see is indistinguishable from God
And serve Him."

Never Fail

a poem for Donald Sultan, on his birthday

That when to be awake was trauma
Then the play of things as they seem
To who had renounced
Desire to manipulate
Could call it life itself.
Then solitude became a new alignment
And
How could the gods not bless
What they had blessed?

Untitled

There is nothing trivial about love.

There is completion in it. And a trial
By pain and power
Barely to be borne.
That fever.

    At its death
There can be rest
And the most grateful of memory.

Passion can bequeath
A truer understanding.

Or its denial
Engender that endless Hour,
Bereft of any Holy Thing,
A bed of thorn
In which we lie with the Banshee.

A New Self-Pity

My friends, and I can not blame them,
Have tired of my woes.
How shall I use this solitude
But in discovery?

That in this, the subspecial case of sorrow in a clown,
The sovereignty of the physician, Time,
Must needs give place to fear of ridicule.
The least abatement in
The differing degrees of woe
Engenders the pathetic need
To leach science from accident.

Mad folk, Sad folk.
In the remedial machinery
Of an unstable world
Of retribution.

Two Minstrels

Two minstrels met in the mortal world
Where they had come to sojourn.
A minstrel boy and a minstrel girl
And to each other did turn.
The each to teach the other songs,
And the other's songs to learn.

"And we may reason, who may not rejoice,"
The one to the other enjoins,
"That we who have made a different choice
Will be paid in different coins.
But I'd trade the fire God put in my voice
For the fire He put in your loins.

"For, Soul of my Soul," the one doth cry,
"I fear it will break my heart,
That I see up ahead the forked way
Which means that we two must part.
And I swear to the Lord I curse the day
I followed this wand'ring Art.

"We are so little time upon the ground
And so near the end of our time.
We are wed to the power in a powerful sound
And the service of the Sublime.
And, surely we will take even love's wound
And betray it into a rhyme."

F.N.S.

A countryside
Suffused with hope
And schooled in thought
Had, by the roadside, one small tree
Which said:
The Queen
Saw her chance and she took the chance to flee.
She packed her bags and fled.
She lives in Southern France.
A bear lies in her bed. The Rose
Inside the luggage she had brought
Is withered. She has tied the bags with rope.
The rope is frayed.
The windowsill is scarred where she has lowered it.

Melamud

Melamud sits in a high-backed chair.
Disturbed by the step on his attic stair,
The creak of the door at his back,
He stops.

He does not acknowledge the polite cough,
And he lowers his eyes again to the text
Till he finishes the paragraph—
Begins to smile by degrees,
And motions his visitor, please
To sit.

Shannon Estuary.
Thirty-Thousand Feet

Lord, who reserved Dominion of the Air
Until the end. Receive the wretched prayer
Of those whose only supportable claim
Is that you have created them. We pray
That you continue to conceal your aim;
That we, in ignorance, conclude our Race.
Let us despoil until the Final Day.
And cry, stupid with fear and arrogance,
Our most haughty confessions of despair,
Our rabid pleas for further sufferance,
Until the tainted soil shall cover us.
Transform to silence our sick susurrus,
And so allow the Earth to bless Thy Name.

A Dream

Up the hill climbing to the Baker's House.
It took more strength than any could suppose
To climb that hill. In dreams, as the hill rose,
My weak lungs heaved, my mouth drew down in
    shame
I prayed for strength and found only self-hate;
Only that constant sickness without name.
For whose mistake was I? Who could abate
My sentence? Who could pardon me?
Who say "We now declare this man is free.
He need not in self-loathing hide his face.
His suffering has not been unobserved—
To the contrary. And the gods he served
Have been defeated in a far-off place.
It was the power of love that broke their thrall.
Therefore rejoice. Bless Him who watches all."

Despite

It did not matter if it was not true.
It matters because it is true.
For though I know I needed
To say it to someone,
I need to say it to you.

Knowing that we cannot,
I thought, "But no, we can."
A vacant folly, save that it is true.
We do not know whether such things will be,
Which rest with God,
But I know it could be,
And write to tell you.

The Blood Chit

Rooting with the Oliver
The moon go in the ground
And we
As we are dedicated.

Oh, Lord, upon Thee
I call.
"Little white paternoster,"
As we all go down.

Adepts
Of the hermetic craft
We have none
Nor
The communality
Of postulants.

Just western longing untold.
And this bond,
"This man
Is an American flyer.
Our consulate
Will pay
Two hundred fifty dollars in gold
For his safe return."

The Hero Pony

Opal in, opal out—
Further blurring the distinction
Between art and decoration,
Stood, not to interpret,
Only to observe,
The Hero Pony—
Fast to his marks.
Flooding, flooding, flooding;
Spotting, no, a donkey not,
And lost the opal.
Wed to the
Decision of his betters, he
Bore it in biding his turn.

Fat man on a long flight,
Short of breath.
The dew point
Told in formula the height
Of clouds of clouds.

Girl in an empty room,
No kindness filled it
With the absent body on the ground.

The beneficent
Perusal of death,
The untaught
Horror of the Philistine,
The vacant musings
Of a vacant mind.

Settled in contemplation,
Steeped in self-contempt;
That balance brought it
Schooled to its marks,
A formula to insure
The correct correspondence between
The dew point and the temperature.
Between the lone girl,
Between the banshee
Vitriol-crazed witch, the tortured child,
The blameless lady fair,
And pampered transportation
Of the fat fellow
From one more-or-less arbitrary point
Unto another in the air.

Below a world of transportation
There is a school of thought.
Slack with surfeit of duty,
Fixed, bleeding, to chocks,
White blinded by lights,
Which we spoke of heretofore—
The difference between art and decoration—
Between the flash of insight
And fidelity to that Wisdom of Yore.

(As preparations
Went on with the calming tread.)

Three streams converged—
Who lives to say that they did not?—
Inside the pony's head.
Which bore
Not toward his death,
But toward the
Quite supportable position
That he never existed.

Who better to
Espouse the one side to the other,
Or
To make the lesser case appear the better?
Like unto the Fakir
Who, obtaining to
That state of bliss
Sufficient to empower him
The Miracle
Ceases forever
To require its prosecution.

Flooding, flooding, flooding, flooding,
Sick that the musing itself
Is an affirmation
Of all that
He was wont to have had in his power to **deny**.

The three degrees of bliss,
The child's shocked
Recognition of betrayal,
And the lover's sigh—

His memory of them as
They replaced the blanket
Round his shoulders.

The moon
Was seen to have rose.
Down from the platform,
Down from high,
Out of the room she goes
To look up at the sky
That held the fat man in the sky.
Out of the light the pony goes.
When it were sentiment
To wish it goodbye—
From which we refrain
Out of an artistic,
Out of an overwrought
Concern for its sensibility.

March 1989

Perhaps you never loved.
That cryptogram.
Stulted by silence, you;
We read in it
Furious meaning. No.

The sick mind races so.
Perhaps you never loved.

Packing

Cruel wind come through the pines.
You followin a deertrack
Where the deertrack winds
You got your eye on it and one eye on the pack.
Thinking of three things, best hope you got them
    right.
One's followin the track
The other is you best have got that horse lasht tight,
The other is that girl you hope when you get back.
Off in the woods sometimes a rabbit track look like a
    moose—
But how would a moose get through that, you see:
N'then the goddamn pack came loose
And the horse shy against a tree
N'goddamn it you could freeze in there now don't you
    know.
Sun goin down, the horse walkt off
The pack all scattered in the snow.
You lasht it wrong. What were you thinkin of
That, back in town—that one hot skinny bitch—
Said, "Isn't this the sweetest love,
Aren't I the best that you could ever find?

And don't you know I know?"
And didn't that get on your mind?
And now you're freezing in the snow.
The mysteries of the Diamond hitch.

The Duck and the Goat

a song for Zaa

An Angora Goat and a Muscovy Duck
Rode to work in a Fire Truck
But the press of traffic and the Laws of Luck
Rendered them late for work.

A Muscovy Duck and an Angora Goat
Sailed back home in a Lobster Boat
They searched the seas for a marker float
In the shape of a Turbanned Turk.

But the Turbanned Turk chafed at his line
And railed at the swell of the Salty Brine
For he pined for the love of a Porcupine
He had seen in the *Ballet Russe*.

And he dreamt of the limelight in Red Square
And her *pas de deux* with a Polar Bear
And he wished to the Lord that he were there.
So he cut his moorings loose.

Lo, the ebb and flow of the Powerful Sea
And the Dreams of Love and Muscovy

And the questioning glance of an Anchovy
Who lay off a black sand Beach.

Where the crystal care of a shining star
Gathered them all from near and far
And set them safe on the black sandbar
To hear the anchovy's speech:

"By the Laws of the Sea and the Law of Chance
And the Timeless Ways of True Romance
And the age-old Customs of the Dance
And by my Office I do declare
That the quillèd Darling of Red Square
Shall quit the enraptured Muscovites' Stare.
As the Turk desires, I shall take him there
To dwell in Peace with his Lady Fair.

"And then to their Homes I shall restore
The Duck and the Goat we have heard of before.
All to prosper and Roam no more,
If that be their delight."

So down to Slumber and down to the Sea.
Our lives of Dance and Minstrelry
Are all in the care of an Anchovy
Who has put it all aright.

And the Polar Bear in single State
Danced to the Plaudits of the Great
And he bows with Dignity and Weight
To wish us the Best Goodnight.

"The Duck and the Goat" is the name of this tale.
It was told to me by a Bobwhite Quail

Who worked as a clerk at the County Jail.
It passed the time till his shift was done;
When we both strolled out in the morning sun
For hot buttered toast and India tea.
And all the prisoners went free.

Warm and Cold

a poem for Willa

It's good to have good clothes on
In which you feel powerful
To be warm when you're cold

To wear something that someone made for you

If you are far away from home
A keepsake will remind you
Of those who love you

You are on a train
Traveling away from them
But they are thinking of you

Through the window you can see
A man going to work
"Inside his house" you think
"There is his family."

In smoke rising you see how cold it is

When you get off the train
They will say how cold it had been
Last week or yesterday.

And I want to sit in the cafe
It's warm there and
The people speak to one another earnestly

The woolens smell of steam

A man can keep
A picture in his heavy shirt.
You can see in his face how well
He remembers what
They all did on that day

He holds the photograph

He puts the photograph away

Zaa

It is not a carved animal
It is a story:
Things by their name.

Blood, or blood running.
One would sit
Quiet as now and say
"I knew him,"
Who knew you.

That road. And some predestined end.
And some to find that friend
And you
To be that friend.

A Christmas Poem

Red shirts for Christmas
Plaid

A new
It, every brings a new ex
Brings a new experience
Of

Under the the be
Beneath the tree a
Shot with gray
A shirt of
Shrinks in the
With *time* it, underneath
The tree, however, wrapped
In twine.

With time, it seems to shrink
Or to grow *more* amenable to
In brown paper
With a card
We all remember the

Or poverty without
But joy with

Though no bicycle
For we

Although in later
Years to be

One can bestow a blessing
This takes thought
Or gift pleasing to see

The mistletoe
The day

If ringing at the door
A bell;

Let us stay,
Warm in our, though

Deep in bed
In thought, in
Slumber have provided for

Those cheeks those
Clothes can make one
Cry and so
What is that, then
But memory

A tree of life
A legacy
A thought
A shirt wrapped in
Brown paper
As they in fact
As they may

They may have
Long ago.

48

A Poem

Storms on the Ocean
Ships on the Sea
Strength to the Masters of the Admiralty.

Strife to the Windward
Calm to the Lee,
But the Wind box'd the compass and blowing free.
Oh, Lord, what will the outcome be?
A dark-eyed girl enchanted me.

A Prophecy

Time unlocks
A season even to be out-of-season.
You will find this note in a tin box
Forty years on.

You will recall you said,
"You are as beautiful as a woman,"
And linen sheets on that bed.
Forty years on.

Here is a poem of love's ways.
Here is a token of length-of-days.
Cast in the form of a prophecy:
That you will come upon
This note, and you will think of me,
Forty years on.

Love Song

Desire must beget desire.
Lord, who knows what peace may be?
But Peace may be the absence of that fire;
Like a sailor swimming in the sea
With never a backward look for his companions.
Like a sailor swimming to the middle of the sea
With never a regret for his companions.

Flying, flying once again
Flying in the face of history.
But, oh, Women, and ah, Men;
Like a sailor, swimming in the sea,
His only thought for his Companion.
Like a sailor swimming to the middle of the sea
Swimming yet with his companion.

A Bargain

I would give my soul
For twenty years of you;
But can not come to barter,
Having lost the one—
Such as it was—
And who can say if I possess the other?

We do not know what time is—
Or longing;
Except we feel the last,
And can not feel the former
Other than in the last.

R.

White flowers dark
Thick eyebrows are a sign
Of great sexual health.
A walk in Westminster
A visage
Which evaporates upon examination.

Vast expanses
Of her soft, flat belly
Her smell on my face
Well. I will push my hands up
Underneath her vest.
No, not now. Later, though,
Right at this instant
Pushing through I saw:
God-sent entitlement,
Long, long adventures,
Sweet friends,
Vagrant hours beyond intensity
Love like a flower falling.

The Brown-Eyed Girl

Ravage, shaking
Once more, love,
Burnt as one ill—
Lips caked dry,
Your limbs shook.
The whites of the eye
Clouded and
I could not keep
My hand still.
Stunned by what I took.

Her sympathy—
We, at the Theater, weep
At that admixture of
Surprise and
Inevitability.

The love of fragrances
Nor random nor inspired
Choice of words
Nor plighted truth of soul
Cannot commemorate
Her sympathy.

The Goshawk

The unfolding of things either inclines
Toward greater or less unity of form,
And never resides in a static state—
Although it may cast that illusion
On anxious souls requiring straight lines.
Which illusion carves so pleasant a norm,
And so correctly curved that it seems straight—
Like a hawk's wing. Like sex as between
Abandoned lovers—things as they may seem.
But from a dispassionate remove, we
Perceive a differing pattern which shuns
All but its own predestined symmetry:
The life of lovers, shaped like not-a-thing,
Finally, but itself—like a hawk's wing.